The *Scottish Salmon* Bible

Claire Macdonald

First published in 2013 by
Birlinn Limited
West Newington House
10 Newington Road
Edinburgh
EH9 1QS

www.birlinn.co.uk

ISBN: 978 1 78027 181 1

British Library Cataloguing-in-Publication Data
A catalogue record for this book is available
from the British Library

Designed and typeset by Mark Blackadder

Printed and bound by Bell & Bain Ltd, Glasgow

Contents

Trout

40 YEARS AGO··
POACHED SALMON & MAYONNAISE

Introduction

Salmon – wild salmon – are one of the miracles of nature. Spawned in a fresh-water pool in a river, salmon – and their delicate relation, sea trout – then swim, once they have reached a level of maturity, far out to the salty sea, returning via some incredible in-built radar system to themselves spawn in the same fresh-water pool in the same river. Their journey is fraught with hazards, chiefly in the form of seals, who maim without necessarily needing to feed on the vulnerable fish.

Wild salmon are a game fish whose taste actually improves if they aren't eaten for two to three days after being caught. This is akin to hanging feathered and furred game. But, for the most part, we who buy salmon buy farmed salmon, and because of the method in which farmed fish are killed, they are best eaten fresh.

Farmed salmon also have no season, whereas for wild salmon the season starts in January and ends towards the end of August.

I choose to buy organically farmed fish because, for one reason, the salmon are more sparsely numbered in the cages in which they live and grow. This means that they can swim against the current and therefore develop muscle tone, which means better texture on the plate.

From a nutritional perspective, salmon should form a regular part of our diet. Some say we should eat salmon at least three times a week. When you read the recipes in this book, you will see that we could eat salmon seven days a week: this wonderful fish is so versatile to the cook that it can be prepared in any number of ways and taste vastly different each time.

Salmon combines deliciously with a wide range of foods and flavours. Forty years ago, or even less, salmon was served either hot with hollandaise sauce or poached and served cold with mayonnaise. Nowadays it is perfectly normal to find salmon served with anything from beetroot and horseradish to cheese and cream. Saffron, as well as other spices, enhance its flavour, and it is complemented by a wide range of foods, including banana, tomato, garlic, ham, bacon and prosciutto – Parma ham – and served with wines, both red and white, and all citrus fruits.

Salmon itself is also varied. We have salmon; hot-smoked salmon, where the fish is smoked and cooked; and cold-smoked salmon, where the fish is smoked but raw (traditionally sold in wafer-thin slices but now also fillets). Salmon can also be cured with sugar, salt and dill to make gravlax, which is usually served with a dill and mustard sauce.

Salmon as a product has come on a long way since its

'hollandaise days' – although this is a perfectly delicious dish, which I feature on p. 71. But mercifully it is no longer sold in 'cutlets', the fish having been sliced through its width, bones and all; these days it appears as fillets, which makes it so very much better both to cook and to eat.

As you will see from the recipes that follow, salmon can be made into a first course or a main course for every possible event or occasion; it suits breakfast as much as a picnic lunch or a celebratory dinner. It is simply a versatile, top-quality food – especially when produced or caught in Scotland.

FENNEL

LEMON

GRAINY MUSTARD

BUTTER

Salmon Tips

- When fresh, salmon can be frozen, but not for very long. After about three weeks its flavour deteriorates (sea trout deteriorates after as little as a few days, if frozen).

- Steam-baking is one of the best and easiest ways to cook salmon, whether fresh or slightly smoked raw fillets: put a sheet of baking parchment onto a baking tray, place the fish on the parchment and strew herbs over it, then season with salt and black pepper (or just black pepper, if the fish is smoked). Cover with another sheet of parchment, making sure the ends are tucked firmly beneath the fish to form a parcel.

- Wild salmon, once it has spawned, is not worth eating. The fish is a deeper shade of coral, almost orange, and its flavour is harsh. Conversely, early season wild salmon is one of life's gastronomic treats!

- Experiment with smoked salmon. Taste salmon smoked by differing smokehouses and buy what appeals to you.

This applies to hot-smoked salmon every bit as much as cold smoked. At Kinloch, we buy from several smokehouses, all with their own identity on the smoke: delicate, such as that from the Sleepy Hollow Smokehouse in Aultbea, Wester Ross; or the strong, peaty smoke of the Hebridean Smokehouse in North Uist. The Smokehouse at Craster in Northumberland is also a favourite, as is the Ullapool Smokehouse.

First Courses

Within this chapter there are recipes for salmon, hot-smoked salmon and slightly smoked raw salmon, in both fillet form and wafer-thin sliced. Some recipes are straightforward first courses, whilst others can be served as a main course. A couple of the recipes are also perfect for picnics. The variety of recipes in this chapter – and the next, Main Courses – clearly demonstrates just how versatile salmon is; in whichever form, it combines so well with so very many different foods and flavours.

Herb crêpes with smoked salmon, cucumber and crème fraîche filling

These crêpes are flavoured with fresh herbs whizzed into the batter. The herbs both look and taste so fresh and complement the filling. In addition, the batter can be made up to 48 hours in advance and stored in the fridge (always remember to stir it up well before making the crêpes). Any leftover batter will also freeze beautifully.

I have demonstrated this recipe on numerous occasions in a variety of locations, from Kinloch to Washington DC. It makes such a good first course.

Serves 6, allowing 2 per person

For the crêpes:
120g (4oz) plain flour
2 large eggs
300ml (½ pint) milk
A handful of parsley, stalks discarded
1 tablespoon snipped chives – they don't break down
    if added whole to the processor
A small handful of dill
1 teaspoon salt
10 grinds of black pepper

For the filling:
½ cucumber, peeled, de-seeded and diced
220g (8oz) smoked salmon, sliced into neat
    dice about thumbnail size

CHIVES

DILL

PARSLEY

300ml (½ pint) crème fraîche
12 grinds of black pepper

Put all the crêpe ingredients into a food processor and whizz till smooth and green-flecked with the herbs. Pour from the processor into a measuring jug and leave to stand for an hour. Give the batter a good stir before making the crêpes.

To cook the crêpes, put a tiny bit of butter – 10g (½oz) – into a non-stick crêpe or omelette pan over a moderately high heat. When the butter is foaming, tipping and tilting the pan, pour in just enough batter to coat the base evenly and thinly. Cook, then when the mixture pulls in slightly from the sides of the pan, slip your thumbs under the crêpe and flip it over to cook on its other side. Slip the crêpe from the pan onto a plastic tray to cool and repeat the process until either you have enough crêpes or have used up all the batter.

For the filling, first peel the cucumber – I use a potato peeler for this. Discard the ends, cut in half, then lengthways, then scoop out the seeds. Chop the remainder into neat dice. Add this to a bowl with the crème fraîche, black pepper and diced smoked salmon.

To assemble, put a spoonful of the smoked salmon mixture in the centre of each crêpe and spread it using the back of a spoon. Roll up into a cigar shape. Put them out onto the plates but loosely cover with cling film to prevent the crêpes from toughening, as the air stales them.

Marinated salmon with smoked salmon, cucumber and pink peppercorns

In this recipe, the salmon is 'cooked' by the acid in the lime juice as it marinates, a process called ceviche, originating in South America. It was devised as a method of preserving fish during its lengthy journey from the coast inland. I like to add smoked salmon to this dish. It makes a very good first course or, in larger amounts, a perfect main course at lunch during hot summer weather. Pink peppercorns, preserved in brine, have a great affinity with all fish and shellfish, but I think above all others the connection is greatest with salmon, in whichever form.

Serves 6

325g (12oz) salmon, skin and bones removed, sliced into
    uniform dice (fingernail size)
Lime or lemon juice, in which to immerse the diced salmon
1 cucumber, peeled, de-seeded and diced
325g (12oz) smoked salmon, cut into similar sized dice as above
2 rounded teaspoons of pink peppercorns, drained – store the
    opened jar of pink peppercorns in the fridge
300ml (½ pint) crème fraîche, which can be reduced fat if you prefer
1 tablespoon of chopped or torn-up dill
No need for salt or pepper in this recipe

Put the diced salmon into a shallow dish and immerse in lime or lemon juice. I suggest you use bottled juice. Leave for 3–4 hours or overnight. Drain off the liquid thoroughly.

Peel the cucumber – I use a potato peeler for this – discarding the ends. Cut into chunks, halving each chunk and scooping out the seeds. Chop the remainder into neat dice.

Put the diced marinated salmon into a bowl and mix in the diced smoked salmon, the diced cucumber, crème fraîche, pink peppercorns and dill. Serve spooned onto each of six plates with, if you like, a clump of salad leaves at the side of each serving.

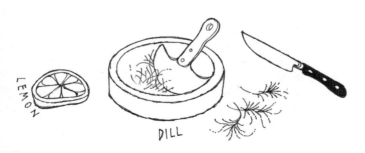

Hot-smoked salmon frittata

A frittata needs very slow cooking. It is a wonderful thing, making a perfect and convenient first course, but a frittata is also useful for a brunch or picnic eating. I like to flake the hot-smoked salmon into a bowl and mix it with the parsley before spooning it into the half-cooked egg mixture. If you prefer not to use the grated parmesan on top, just leave it out.

Serves 6

25g (1oz) butter
6 large eggs
1 teaspoon salt
About 12 grinds of black pepper
2 tablespoons cold water
A dash of Tabasco – leave this out if you really dislike chilli
220g (8oz) hot-smoked salmon, flaked from the skin
2 rounded tablespoons finely chopped parsley
50g (2oz) grated parmesan

Put a non-stick omelette pan measuring about 20cm (8in.) diameter on a low heat and add in the butter. Beat together the eggs with the salt, pepper, cold water and Tabasco. When the butter has melted, pour in the beaten egg mixture and leave to cook very gently – should the mixture rise slightly up the sides of the pan, the frittata is cooking too quickly. Reduce the heat beneath the pan and be patient. The base cooking should take 7–8 minutes. Meanwhile, put on your grill to half heat. When the base is cooked approximately halfway up, fork the salmon and parsley mixture evenly over the surface and into the soft egg. Scatter the grated parmesan over the surface and put the pan under the grill. Watch as it slowly cooks from the top down. Shake the pan gently to test when the frittata is cooked – when the egg mixture beneath and around the salmon no longer wobbles.

Take the pan out from under the grill and leave to stand for 5–10 minutes. Then slip it from the pan onto a warm serving plate and slice to serve. A frittata doesn't need to be served hot, straight from the pan; it is just as good cooled. But it must be made the same day that it is to be eaten.

Smoked salmon with walnut butter brown bread roulades

This is a way to serve the best-quality smoked salmon just as it is, but accompanied by a delicious slightly crunchy bread roulade. It is simple to create and can be made several hours in advance. Most convenient! However, they must be covered with cling film till it is time to eat.

Serves 6

12 slices of smoked salmon – or 18, if your planned main
    course is fairly light in content
3 lemons – for quartering to serve beside the smoked salmon

For the brown bread roulade:
1 tablespoon olive oil
120g (4oz) chopped walnuts
1 level teaspoon salt
175g (6oz) soft butter
8 slices of brown bread, crusts sliced off

Put the olive oil into a saucepan on a moderate heat. Fry the chopped walnuts with the salt stirred in, then crush the nuts to make them more like large crumbs. Fry and stir for 7–8 minutes, then take the pan off the heat and cool the walnuts. In a bowl, beat the soft butter, then add the cooled fried walnuts.

On a sheet of baking parchment, using a rolling pin, roll each crustless slice of bread until it is thinner. Spread each with the walnut butter and roll up lengthways, pressing each firmly. Slice each roulade in half, so that you end up with 16 roulades, allowing two each with some over. Cover the plate of walnut butter bread roulades with cling film until required.

Smoked salmon mousse-filled smoked salmon parcels

I realise that you can buy items which resemble this recipe in some supermarkets, but I assure you that when you make your own you will see there is a vast difference. Invariably, the bought smoked salmon parcels are made from poorer quality salmon in order to keep the price down. Make your own every time – they are better for you and just taste so much better.

The quantities may sound small but they make just the right amount, I think. Especially if they are to be followed by a main course and a pud!

Serves 6

6 slices of smoked salmon, each weighing 150–175g (5–6oz)
3 more slices of smoked salmon, each weighing 150–175g (5–6oz)
4 leaves of gelatine soaked in cold water for 10 minutes
300ml (½ pint) vegetable stock, warmed
A dash of Tabasco
1 tablespoon lemon juice
1 teaspoon anchovy sauce
About 12 grinds of black pepper
300ml (½ pint) single cream
1 large egg white

Put six scone-cutters or similar (diameter 4cm/2½in.) onto a baking tray lined with baking parchment. Line each scone-cutter with a slice of smoked salmon, which should overhang the edges.

Meanwhile, lift the soaked gelatine from its cold water and drop it into the warm stock. Stir to dissolve completely and leave till cold and starting to gel.

Put the three slices of smoked salmon into a food processor with the gelling stock and whizz, adding the dash of Tabasco, the tablespoon of lemon juice, the anchovy sauce and the black pepper. Lastly, briefly whizz in the single cream. Tip this into a bowl.

In a clean bowl, whisk up the egg white till stiff and fold this quickly and thoroughly through the smoked salmon mixture. Spoon this into the smoked salmon-lined metal rounds and cover with the bit of overhanging smoked salmon.

Leave in a cool place to set for several hours – these can be made a day in advance.

Before serving, lift off the metal rings, then carefully lift up each parcel and lay face down on a serving plate so that the sliced smoked salmon is uppermost. Serve with crispy melba toast.

Potted salmon with walnuts and lemon

This is an excellent way to use up leftover salmon from a hot or cold main course. The fish is bound with melted butter and the fried chopped walnuts, combined with the flavour of the grated lemon and a small amount of its juice, complement the taste of the fish so well. This is an excellent first course, nicest eaten with crunchy melba toast, but because of the butter content it is wise to plan a fairly light main course to follow. An alternative is to serve the potted salmon as a light main course for lunch or supper, accompanied by a mixed leaf salad.

Serves 6

375g (12oz) butter
1 tablespoon olive oil
1 teaspoon salt
About 15 grinds of black pepper
75g (3oz) chopped walnuts
450g (1lb) cooked salmon, flaked and any bones and skin removed
Finely grated rind of 1 lemon and 1 tablespoon of lemon juice
1 tablespoon finely chopped parsley

Start by clarifying the butter. Let it melt very slowly in a saucepan, but not on direct heat. The curdy part will settle on the bottom of the pan whilst the clarified butter rests on top. When melted, and carefully poured, the curds remain on the bottom of the pan. Clarifying butter really is that easy!

In a separate pan, heat the olive oil, stirring in the salt and black pepper. Fry the chopped walnuts on a moderately high heat for 5–7 minutes, moving them constantly so that they fry evenly. Set aside to cool.

Put the flaked cold salmon into a food processor. Whizz, adding half the amount of clarified butter, the grated lemon rind and a tablespoon of lemon juice. Scrape the contents of the processor into a bowl and mix in the cooled fried walnuts and the chopped parsley. Mix very well.

Divide evenly between six small ramekins, smooth the surface of each and pour the remainder of the clarified butter on each ramekin to seal in the potted salmon and walnuts beneath. Cover each ramekin with cling film and store in the fridge for up to two days, being sure to take the ramekins up to room temperature half an hour before serving. Remove the cling film before serving.

NOT CLARIFIED BUTTER·· WORRY WORRY SCREAM!

Curry-rubbed baked salmon with caramelised bananas

This may sound odd, but I assure you that it is delicious! Caramelising the bananas is easiest done using a powerful blow torch, but you can grill them if you do not possess one. I serve this warm, but not very hot straight from the oven.

Serves 6

175g (6oz) soft butter
3 rounded teaspoons medium-strength curry powder
1 teaspoon salt
6 pieces of filleted salmon, each weighing about 4oz/120g
6 bananas

In a bowl mix together the soft butter, the curry powder and the salt. Divide this evenly between the salmon, rubbing it into the surface of the fish. Put each piece onto a non-stick tray and bake in a moderate heat (350°F/180°C/gas 4) for 10–15 minutes.

Meanwhile, peel the bananas and slice them in half on the diagonal (if the bananas are very large, just use three and slice each in four slices). Put the bananas onto a baking tray and either grill them beneath a half-hot grill, turning over once speckled golden brown, or blast them with a blow torch held about 20cm/8in. away so as not

to scorch them, again blow-torching until they speckle
golden brown.

To serve, put a piece of baked curried salmon onto
each of six warmed plates, adding two slices of
caramelised banana beside each piece of fish.

Hot-smoked salmon salad with apple, horseradish and crème fraîche dressing

This makes an excellent first course — and this amount will feed four people as a main course salad. It's a perfect lunch or supper in warm weather, however, it is an ideal first course any time of the year.

Serves 6

675g (1½lb) hot-smoked salmon, flaked from skin
Assorted salad leaves — some watercress is good amongst them, the peppery taste complementing that of both the hot-smoked salmon and the dressing

For the dressing:
3 eating apples, peeled and grated
2 tablespoons lemon juice
300ml (½ pint) crème fraîche, which can be half-fat if you choose
1 rounded tablespoon horseradish — I use Colman's, or the Co-op's own brand is very good, too
1 rounded tablespoon finely chopped parsley
I don't think any salt or pepper is necessary in this dressing

---

In a bowl, grate the apples and immediately mix in the lemon juice — this is to help prevent the apples from discolouring, though it is there for taste, too. Add the

crème fraîche, horseradish and finely chopped parsley
and mix together well.

Divide the salad leaves between each of six plates
(four, if this is to be a main course) and then divide the
flaked hot-smoked salmon evenly between the plates.
Lastly, put a spoonful of dressing on top of the flaked
hot-smoked salmon.

34

Salmon and dill cream tart

This recipe – like so many others – has history.

I devised it many years ago when – extraordinarily – I was one of the top three in a picnic competition run by Krug champagne. The finals took place on the riverbank at Henley. I turned up with my salmon and dill tart, a

bowl of salad, a rug, a jug of roses and my pud, which was a lemony-strawberry concoction, if I remember rightly. This was my idea of a perfect picnic for a special occasion – but I was heavily outclassed by the other two finalists, both chefs of high repute, who arrived with portable gas ovens and stage props for their picnics that put my jug of roses to shame (I remember hat stands with boaters and arrays of garden furniture being brought from vans). I knew I could only come last in the pecking order as I watched one chef spinning sugar over his elaborate pud, whilst the other was stuffing boned-out duck! But it was all part of life's rich tapestry and great fun – and Michel Roux (senior) kissed me on the cheek! I didn't want to wash my face afterwards!

I also made this tart recently for a very special 40th birthday, when I was doing a cooking demo for the birthday girl in Essex and I believe it has stood the test of time. It is simple and delicious, and makes a perfect first course, as well as being good picnic eating!

Serves 6

For the pastry – to line a metal flan dish 22cm/9in. diameter
120g (4oz) butter, cut into bits and hard from the fridge
175g (6oz) plain flour
1 rounded teaspoon icing sugar
1 teaspoon salt
About 12 grinds of black pepper

For the filling:
675g (1½lb) salmon, either plain or slightly smoked raw fillets.
2 large eggs, 2 large egg yolks
300ml (½ pint) single cream
Level teaspoon salt
About 15 grinds of black pepper
A grating of nutmeg
25g (1oz) dill, torn in feathery fronds, stalks discarded

For the pastry, put the butter, flour, icing sugar and seasoning into a food processor and whizz to fine crumbs. Press these firmly over the base and up the sides of the flan tin – there is no need to butter or oil the flan tin before pressing in the pastry crumbs – then put this into the fridge for at least an hour. Bake straight from the fridge on a moderate heat (350°F/180°C/gas 4) for 20 minutes. The sides of the pastry may slip a bit towards the base; with a metal spoon, scrape this firmly back into place. Allow to cool.

Dice the salmon, discarding the skin, into pieces about 1cm in size. Arrange evenly over the base of the cooled pastry. Beat the two eggs and two egg yolks together well, then add the cream. Mix the salt, pepper and nutmeg through this mixture and pour this in amongst the salmon. Scatter the torn-up dill fronds over the surface and bake in the same moderate heat as for the pastry for about 25 minutes or until, when the tart is gently shaken, the filling no longer wobbles.

I serve this tart tepid and it cuts perfectly into slices.

Hot-smoked salmon with shaved fennel and pink grapefruit with chive dressing

This is such a useful and light first course. Although no salmon is light to eat, it being rather filling, there is nothing rich about this dish. I leave the pieces of hot-smoked salmon whole rather than flaking them.

Serves 6

6 pieces of hot-smoked salmon, each weighing about 120g (4oz), skin removed
2 bulbs of fennel, trimmed at top and bottom
3 pink grapefruit

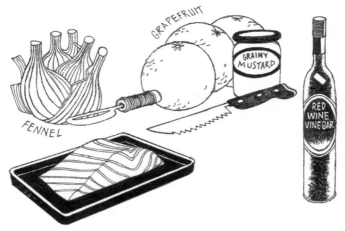

For the dressing:
2 teaspoons grainy mustard
1 teaspoon salt
About 10 grinds of black pepper
1 tablespoon red wine vinegar
4 tablespoons extra virgin olive oil
1 rounded tablespoon of very thinly sliced chives

———————————

Slice the fennel bulbs as thinly as you possibly can – I use my potato peeler but, if you have one, a mandolin is perfect for the task. Alternatively, a steady hand and a very sharp knife will do the trick!

With a serrated knife, remove the skin and white pith from each of the pink grapefruit. Then, cutting in towards the centre of each grapefruit, slice between the pith, leaving pith-less segments. Put the finely sliced fennel and the grapefruit segments into a bowl.

Make the dressing by mixing all the ingredients together very thoroughly, adding in the finely sliced chives last. Pour the dressing into the bowl with the fennel and pink grapefruit and mix through.

To assemble, put a piece of hot-smoked salmon on each of the six plates and encircle each piece of fish with a spoonful of salad.

Hot-smoked salmon and avocado terrine

This is an excellent terrine to serve as a first course; it is fairly filling, so plan for a lighter main course to follow. Alternatively, it can form part of a buffet – perfect, because it can be eaten using only a fork, no need for a knife. A word of caution, though: I like to make this in a Pyrex or china terrine dish rather than a metal one, as metal tends to discolour the avocado, even through the cling film that lines the tin.

Serves 6 (generously)

300ml (½ pint) vegetable stock
5 leaves of gelatine soaked in cold water for 10 minutes
450g (1lb) hot-smoked salmon, flaked and the skin discarded
2 rounded tablespoons of finely chopped parsley and chives, mixed
1 teaspoon salt
About 15 grinds of black pepper
3 avocados
2 tablespoons lemon juice
1 teaspoon Tabasco
300ml (½ pint) crème fraîche

Line the terrine dish with a double thickness of cling film, taking care to push it gently into each corner. I find using a small wodge of kitchen paper just the thing to ease it in.

Heat the stock and when it is warm drop the soaked gelatine leaves into it, stirring to be sure that the gelatine dissolves completely in the hot liquid. Set to one side to cool completely.

FLICK OUT THE AVOCADO STONES

Pour half of the gelatine stock into a bowl with the flaked salmon, mixing in the finely chopped parsley and chives, the salt and black pepper.

Cut each avocado in half and flick out the stones. Scoop out the flesh and put into a food processor. Whizz, adding the lemon juice, Tabasco and the remainder of the gelling stock. Lastly, briefly whizz in the crème fraîche.

Put half this mixture into the bottom of the lined terrine – bang gently to dislodge any air bubbles – and leave in a cool place until just set. Spoon the herbs and flaked hot-smoked salmon over the set layer of avocado and put the remainder of the avocado mixture over the top. Bang gently once more to dislodge any air bubbles, then cover with cling film. Leave in a cool place for several hours to set. I tend to make this in the morning for serving the same evening.

To serve, remove the cover of cling film, invert the terrine and slowly peel back the bottom layer of cling film. Cut into 1cm thick slices to serve.

41

Thai salmon patties with cucumber yogurt dressing

These make such a good first course, and seem to be loved by children as well as by adults. The patties can be made a day in advance. They are good served just warm, rather than hot, straight from the pan. If you make them smaller, they make a good canapé, too, with a dab of the dressing on top of each.

Serves 6

For the salmon patties:
900g (2lb) salmon, skin and bones removed, cut into small chunks
2 spring onions, trimmed at either end and sliced
Finely grated rind of 1 lime and its juice
A piece of fresh ginger about 2in./4cm long, skin sliced off
    and finely diced
1 tablespoon sweet chilli sauce
1 tablespoon soy sauce
Handful of coriander
Light olive oil for frying the patties

For the dressing:
300ml (½ pint) natural yogurt
1 cucumber, peeled, de-seeded and diced
Finely grated rind of 1 lime and its juice
1 teaspoon salt

Put the salmon chunks into a food processor with the sliced spring onions, the lime rind and the diced ginger. Whizz, adding the lime juice, the sweet chilli sauce, the soy sauce and the coriander. Scrape the salmon mixture into a bowl, cover and put into the fridge for about an hour.

While the patties are chilling, peel the skin from the cucumber – I use a potato peeler – and slice off either end. Cut the peeled cucumber into lengths of about 4cm (2in.) and cut each in half. Scoop away the seeds, then slice the halves into neat dice.

Tip the yogurt into a bowl and add the diced cucumber, the finely grated rind and juice of the lime, and the salt, and stir together thoroughly.

To make the patties, first dampen your hands with cold water. Divide the salmon mixture into even-sized

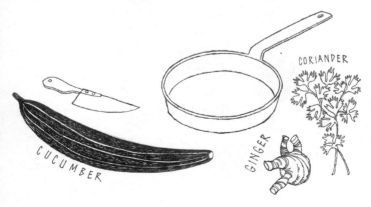

CORIANDER

CUCUMBER

GINGER

small balls, about golf-ball size, and flatten. Put the patties onto a parchment-lined tray.

Heat 2–3 tablespoons of olive oil in a non-stick sauté pan and fry the patties for 2–3 minutes on moderately high heat, turning them over to fry on their other side for the same amount of time. Lift them from the pan onto several thicknesses of absorbent kitchen paper to absorb some of the oil.

Serve warm, with the dressing to one side.

Salmon and streaky bacon skewers with chilli aioli

These make a delicious first course but served in larger amounts they can be just as good as a main course. The chilli aioli can be made a couple of days in advance of eating, but keep it in a covered bowl in the fridge until required. I use wooden skewers, but I soak them in cold water for an hour before sticking the bacon-wrapped chunks of salmon onto them, then grill or barbecue.

Serves 6

900g (2lb) salmon cut into chunks about 2cm (1in.) in size –
 you should have 36
12 rashers of thinly cut dry-cured unsmoked streaky bacon

For the aioli:
1 large egg, plus 1 large egg yolk
2 fat cloves of garlic, blanched twice
1 teaspoon salt
15 grinds of black pepper
1 teaspoon caster sugar
½ teaspoon dried chilli flakes
300ml (½ pint) olive oil
2 tablespoons lemon juice
1 tablespoon white wine vinegar

Start by blanching the garlic cloves in their skins, i.e. put into cold water, bring to the boil and drain off, then repeat. This eliminates the harsh, raw taste.

To make the aioli, break the egg into a food processor and add the yolk, the blanched garlic, the salt and black pepper, and the sugar and chilli flakes. Whizz, adding the olive oil, drop by drop, until you have an emulsion, then add the rest of the olive oil in a very thin, steady trickle. When all the oil is incorporated, add the lemon juice and white wine vinegar. Scrape the aioli into a bowl, cover and store in the fridge until you are ready to serve it.

For the salmon skewers, lay each rasher of bacon on a board and stroke its length with a large knife – this enlarges each rasher by at least half its length again. Cut each into three even lengths. Wrap each bit of salmon in streaky bacon and stick it onto a soaked skewer.

These are perfect for the barbecue, in which case, when the coals have died down to white heat, put the skewers onto the grill for 2–3 minutes. Then turn and repeat on the other side.

In the absence of a barbecue, heat your grill. Cover the grill pan with foil – to avoid needing to scrub it during washing-up afterwards – and put the skewers onto this. Grill until the bacon turns crisp, then turn over and grill on the other side. The bacon prevents the salmon from drying out as it cooks.

Serve with a small clump of salad leaves, if you like, with the aioli handed out separately.

Hot-smoked salmon, bacon and garlic pâté

I have included this recipe in the section on first courses, but this coarse-textured pâté can also be used as a luxurious filling for buns if you are planning an elaborate winter or summer picnic. In 2012, on a chilly November day during our celebratory weekend to mark the 40th anniversary of Kinloch, we ate this pâté in buns, accompanied by spicy butternut squash soup, around a bonfire for our picnic lunch!

NOVEMBER BONFIRE AT KINLOCH

Serves 6

400g (13oz) low-fat cream cheese
375g (12oz) hot-smoked salmon, flaked and the skin removed
6 rashers of dry-cured streaky bacon, grilled till crisp, cooled,
    then broken into bits
About 15 grinds of black pepper – no need for salt in this recipe –
    the bacon contributes enough saltiness for most palates
2 tablespoon finely chopped parsley
2 fat cloves of garlic, blanched

First, blanche the garlic cloves in their skins twice, i.e. put into cold water, bring to the boil and drain off, then repeat. This eliminates the harsh, raw taste – it really is worth the minimal effort of doing this.

Tip the cream cheese into a mixing bowl. Add the flaked hot-smoked salmon, the bacon, the chopped parsley and the black pepper. Snip the top off each blanched garlic clove and the skins will slip off easily. Crush each garlic clove and add to the contents of the bowl. Mix thoroughly, then put the 'pâté' into a bowl to serve. This works well with either warm seeded bread or rolls, or with melba toast or oatcakes.

Smoked salmon with Avruga and crème fraîche

This is the simplest of first courses, but the tastes go together so very well. It is my ideal first course for a special occasion. Avruga is the grainy roe of herring – as opposed to the soft roes. It is a world more delicious than lumpfish roe and can be bought in small- or medium-sized jars, from specialist delis (House of Bruar stock it). A jar in the fridge (keeping an eye on the use-by date) is a real standby for those times when something out of the ordinary is called for with very little notice.

12 slices of the best-quality smoked salmon
6 tablespoons Avruga
300ml (½ pint) crème fraîche – this can be half-fat
About 12 grinds of black pepper – no need for salt, as both the
    Avruga and smoked salmon contribute sufficient saltiness for
    most palates
1 tablespoon finely chopped parsley

In a bowl, stir the Avruga into the crème fraîche, then add the finely chopped parsley and black pepper. Put two slices of smoked salmon on each of six plates and spoon the Avruga crème fraîche in even amounts – about a tablespoon – beside or on top of the fish, whichever you prefer. Serve buttered brown bread, crusts cut off, to accompany the dish.

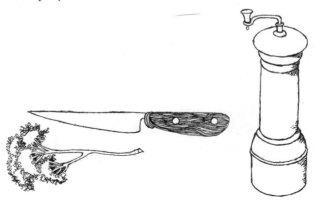

Smoked salmon, with cream cheese and chive filling

This is the simplest but most luxurious filling for sandwiches or bagels for a special occasion. These days we can buy smoked salmon anywhere, yet still a really excellent smoked salmon is a luxury. Be generous with your filling and nothing can really beat this, accompanied by a glass of cold but not over-chilled white wine (my preference is for a northern Italian sauvignon blanc, from Friuli, produced by the Tonello family and available from Corney & Barrow). Utterly delicious!

Serves 6

450g (1lb) half-fat cream cheese
1 level tablespoon very neatly chopped fresh chives (beware those that have been picked for several days, as they taste too strong)
About 20 grinds of black pepper
Finely grated rind of 1 lemon and the juice of half the lemon
450g (1lb) best-quality smoked salmon

Tip the cream cheese into a bowl and beat into it the chives, black pepper, finely grated lemon rind and juice. Slice and dice the smoked salmon – it is so much easier to make this way, rather than using slices of smoked salmon without dicing them. Tip into the cream cheese mixture.

Whether you butter the bagels, brown bread or seeded rolls is up to you, but this should fill six adequately. If you would like any salad leaves, opt for watercress; I feel it has a special taste affinity with smoked salmon; in fact, with all types of salmon, for that matter.

Crostini

Crostini are small, dried rather than toasted pieces of
French bread and work well with interesting salmon
combinations on top. You can use small oatcakes, if you
prefer; the cocktail-sized ones made by Nairn's are
perfect. Crostini make such a good first course in the
hand, with no need for plates, knives or forks, just
napkins. Alternatively, crostini can be served as canapés
with drinks. They are versatile and do not need to be
made at the last minute.

Here are three different toppings for salmon crostini,
each making enough for six people, allowing three per
person.

Smoked salmon with horseradish butter and dill

120g (4oz) soft butter
1 rounded teaspoon horseradish
2 teaspoons lemon juice
10 grinds of black pepper
220g (8oz) smoked salmon, sliced into thin strips about 1cm wide
Dill fronds – not just for garnish; an integral part of the flavour
    overall, too

In a bowl, beat together the soft butter, horseradish,
lemon juice and black pepper. Spread a small amount of

this butter on each of the 18 crostini or mini oatcakes and spiral a thin strip of smoked salmon on each. Finish off with a dill frond on top.

Pea and mint puree with hot-smoked salmon and pea-shoot garnish

220g (8oz) frozen petit pois, thawed completely
6 mint leaves, preferably applemint, which has the best flavour
2 tablespoons crème fraîche
½ teaspoon salt
10 grinds of black pepper
175g (6oz) hot-smoked salmon, flaked from the skin
18 pea shoots

Put the petit pois into a saucepan and pour boiling water over them. Over a high heat, bring them to the boil, count to ten, then drain. Run cold water through the peas. Tip them into a food processor with the mint leaves, salt and black pepper, and whizz. Lastly, very briefly whizz in the two tablespoons of crème fraîche. Scrape this mixture into a bowl and mix in the flaked hot-smoked salmon. Divide this between 18 crostini or mini oatcakes and put a pea shoot on top of each.

Salmon pâté with quails' eggs

9 quails' eggs
220g (8oz) leftover cold poached salmon
3 anchovy fillets, drained of their preserving oil
220g (8oz) cream cheese, which can be half-fat, if you prefer
10 grinds of black pepper
1 tablespoon finely chopped parsley

Boil the quails' eggs for five minutes, then drain. Run cold water through the eggs in their saucepan before removing the shells and cutting each in half lengthways.

Put the salmon into a food processor with the anchovy fillets, cream cheese and black pepper. Whizz until smooth. Add the parsley at the very end, whizz briefly, just to mix it through, then scrape this into a bowl.

Spread the mixture on each of 18 crostini or mini oatcakes. Finish off with half a quail's egg, yolk uppermost.

Main Courses

Salmon, in all its different guises, is a real standby for all occasions. It freezes for a limited length of time – two months at the outside – where other fish aren't so successful (sea trout for example). Salmon is so varied, and so good for us from a nutritional aspect that we can and should eat it at least three times a week. That is no problem whatsoever when you think of all the different ways it can be cooked and served up. And salmon truly is fast food – which is convenience cooking at its very best.

In this chapter, I've chosen recipes for all occasions and eventualities, from a quick stir-fry for a family supper to the double salmon fish pie. When a special occasion presents itself, coulibiac is ideal or the luxurious salmon, cream and spinach stew, scented with saffron. There are so many other recipes besides these, suitable for all occasions – lunch, supper or a more special dinner.

Poached salmon, served cold with mayonnaise

It seems right to start this section on main courses with the best-known way to serve salmon or sea trout during the summer months – poached, served cold, with a good plain mayonnaise as accompaniment. Yet the simple skills used in this dish are often found lacking by chefs in some usually very good establishments. One of my biggest disappointments was when my mother ordered it at a hotel in the Lake District where we had booked lunch for our large family to celebrate her 90th birthday. She chose cold poached salmon with mayonnaise and what was served was a positive disgrace. As soon as possible, however, following the great birthday lunch, I cooked her and my father a proper poached cold salmon, with a good mayonnaise, hoping to compensate for the birthday disaster.

An elderly Scottish cook, Mrs Bell, who lived in our village of Tunstall in Lancashire, taught me this method some 50 years ago (gulp! Can it be that long? But it is!) and it is infallible.

Before poaching the salmon, you must first prepare a court bullion.

Serves 6

900g–1.3kg (2–3lb) salmon

For the court bouillon:
1.8l (3 pints) water
1 onion, skinned and halved
4 sticks of celery, washed and broken
1 teaspoon bashed black peppercorns
2 teaspoons salt
A handful of crushed parsley stalks – crushing releases the flavour
Juice of 2 lemons

Put all the above ingredients into a large saucepan and bring to the boil, then simmer gently, uncovered, for 35–40 minutes. Take the pan off the heat and cool, then strain the bouillon. Throw away the vegetables, etc.
Put the salmon in a wide pan (no need for a fish kettle itself, unless you are cooking a whole, large salmon – in such a case, if you don't own a fish kettle, anyone who does will willingly lend it to you). Pour the cold bouillon over the fish – if it doesn't actually cover the fish, add cold water till it does; the piece of salmon must be immersed in the liquid.

Put the pan onto a moderately high heat and bring the liquid to a rolling bubble. Boil for exactly one minute, then lift the pan off the heat and cool the salmon completely in the liquid. This applies to any weight of salmon, as the cooking time adjusts according to the weight. The larger the piece of salmon, the longer the liquid will take to reach boiling point, and also the longer it will take to grow cold. Hence the fact that the salmon, no matter how large, will be perfectly cooked to serve cold if you follow the above guideline.

For the mayonnaise:
1 large egg, plus one large egg yolk
1 rounded teaspoon caster sugar
1 rounded teaspoon salt
About 12 grinds of black pepper
1 rounded teaspoon Dijon mustard
300ml (½ pint) olive oil
3 tablespoons white wine vinegar – start with two,
    then add the third if taste dictates

Put the egg, the yolk, the sugar, salt, pepper and Dijon mustard into a food processor. Whizz, then add the oil – still whizzing – drop by drop, till you have an emulsion. At this point, add in the oil in a thin, steady trickle. When all the oil is incorporated, add two tablespoons of white wine vinegar, taste, and add the third if necessary. If you want to thin down the mayonnaise, whizz in two tablespoons of milk. This will keep for up to three days in the fridge.

When the salmon is cold, carefully lift it out and peel off the skin from either side before serving with the mayonnaise. If you like, garnish with wafer-thin sliced cucumber in overlapping layers.

Salmon with lemon, parsley, chilli and garlic spaghetti

This is one of our favourite ways to eat salmon with spaghetti. Both are simple to prepare and very quick to cook – literally in the seven minutes it takes to boil the water around the cooking spaghetti. This is packed with punchy flavours and the result is really very good.

Serves 6

375g (12oz) spaghetti
900g (2lb) filleted salmon, skin removed and the fish sliced
    into fairly small dice
Finely grated rind of 2 lemons
2 rounded tablespoons finely chopped parsley
3 fat cloves of garlic, blanched twice
½ teaspoon dried chilli flakes
8 tablespoons extra virgin olive oil
1 teaspoon salt

Boil the spaghetti in salted water for seven minutes. While the pasta is cooking, thoroughly mix the remaining ingredients together in a bowl.

Drain the spaghetti and return it to the saucepan. Add the contents of the bowl to the pan on a low to moderate heat and fork together for 2–3 minutes – the heat from the drained pasta cooks the diced salmon.

Serve immediately into warmed plates or bowls.

Slightly smoked salmon with dill and crème fraîche spaghetti

This is another of my favourite ways to combine spaghetti with salmon, but this recipe calls for slightly smoked fillets of salmon as opposed to the previous recipe, which uses plain salmon, unsmoked. I really have to give credit for this dish to my eldest daughter, Alexandra, whose concoction it is. Living as she does in rural Bavaria, she has access for the most part only to fresh-water fish; those of us lucky enough to live as we do – surrounded by sea, with the best sea fish and shellfish anywhere in the world – know this is very 'second best' in the fish-eating stakes! But she can and does buy imported salmon, both smoked and unsmoked.

___

Serves 6

375g (12oz) spaghetti
675g (1½lb) slightly smoked salmon fillets, sliced into
    thumbnail-sized dice
300ml (½ pint) crème fraîche, which can be half-fat
A handful of dill, coarsely chopped
About 15 grinds of black pepper – no need for salt, as the slightly
    smoked salmon provides enough saltiness for most palates

___

Boil the spaghetti in salted water for seven minutes. While the pasta is cooking, mix the remaining ingredients together in a bowl. As soon as the spaghetti's ready, drain it and tip it back into its saucepan. With the pan on a low heat, stir the contents of the bowl into the pasta, forking it through for a couple of minutes. This allows the salmon to cook in the heat of the spaghetti.

Serve immediately.

Filo parcels of salmon, tomato and basil

I ate this delicious main course many years ago when judging a competition for young chefs. The chef who created this, Ross Spence, is now a not-so-young chef, working in his father's wonderful hotel, the Marcliffe at Pitfodels. This is my version of his winning dish – he was head and shoulders above the rest of the competitors even then, some 15 years ago.

This recipe can be prepared in advance of baking by 4–5 hours.

Serves 6

6 pieces of filleted salmon, each weighing about 175g (6oz)
6 sheets of filo pastry
75g (3oz) butter, melted

For the basil and tomato mixture:
6 ripe tomatoes, skinned, halved, seeds scooped out and
    chopped finely
A handful of basil leaves
Finely grated rind of 1 lemon
1 teaspoon salt
About 15 grinds of black pepper
2 tablespoons olive oil

Stab each tomato in two or three places and dip into boiling water, speared on the end of a fork. Then peel off their skins. Cut in half, scoop out the seeds and finely chop the remaining flesh. Chop the basil leaves (I know this will discolour them a bit, but it doesn't matter because the discolouring won't be discernible in the tomato mixture). In a bowl, combine the basil and tomatoes, adding the grated lemon rind, salt, black pepper and olive oil. Mix thoroughly.

Lay a sheet of filo on a work surface and brush completely with melted butter. Cover with a second sheet of filo and brush this, too, with melted butter. Cut this double sheet of buttered filo in half widthways. Put a piece of salmon in the middle of each half. Add a spoonful of tomato mixture on top of each piece of salmon, spreading it with the back of the spoon. Fold the filo over each piece of salmon, making a neat parcel. Brush each all over with melted butter and put the parcels onto a non-stick baking sheet.

If you prepare these in advance of baking by even as little as half an hour, loosely cover the parcels on the baking sheet with cling film.

Remove the cling film and bake in a hot oven (450°F/220°C/gas 7) for 15 minutes. Serve immediately.

Salmon, bacon and leek macaroni cheese

Throughout this book you will find bacon or Parma ham appearing as an ingredient. The combination of pork, whether in the form of ham or bacon, with fish – in these cases with salmon – is one of the most extraordinary of taste combinations. But it works so well.

In this recipe, strips of dry-cured back bacon (unsmoked) fried with leeks and garlic make a delicious sauce in which the small pieces of salmon cook, when baked with the macaroni – one of those lunch or supper dishes where the protein (salmon) and vegetables (leeks) and starch (macaroni) are all in one delicious dish. Whether you choose to use plain salmon or slightly smoked fillets of salmon is up to you!

Serves 6

220g (8oz) macaroni or penne pasta, boiled in salted water
    for 7 minutes then drained
50g (2oz) butter
1 tablespoon olive oil
1 onion, finely diced
3 rashers unsmoked back bacon – snip off the fat with scissors
    and slice into strips 1cm wide
4 medium-sized leeks, weighing about 450g (1lb) when
    trimmed at either end, sliced diagonally (approx. 1cm wide)
1 fat clove of garlic, finely diced

2 fairly level tablespoons plain flour
900ml (1½ pints) milk
1 level teaspoon salt
About 15 grinds of black pepper
A grating of nutmeg
150g (6oz) grated cheddar cheese – I use Mull cheddar for
    this and for most recipes requiring cheddar cheese
4 pieces of filleted salmon, diced about 1cm in size

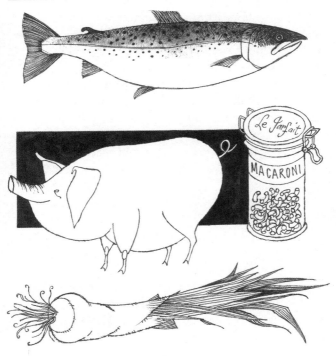

Melt the butter and heat the olive oil together in a wide, large saucepan. Over moderately high heat fry the onion and the bacon, stirring occasionally, for 3–4 minutes. Add the leeks, trimmed and sliced on the diagonal approx. 1cm wide. It seems a fairly large amount, but, as they fry, for about 6–7 minutes, the leeks wilt right down. When they are soft, stir in the flour, adding the garlic at this time too. Cook the flour for a minute before gradually adding the milk, stirring continuously. When the sauce begins to bubble gently, draw the pan off the heat and stir in the salt, black pepper and nutmeg. Add in 75g (3oz) of grated cheddar and the diced salmon.

While you are making the sauce, boil the pasta. When it is cooked, drain and stir it into the hot sauce immediately. Tip the contents of the saucepan into an ovenproof dish (I would recommend about two litres volume). Scatter the remaining grated cheddar evenly over the entire surface and grill at two-thirds heat. Watch in case of burning!

The dish is ready when the cheese turns golden brown.

This is good with a spinach and tomato salad as an accompaniment, although none is actually necessary.

NB You can make the whole dish in advance by several hours, in which case reheat in a high temperature (400°F/200°C/gas 6) until the cheese melts on the surface and the contents bubble gently beneath the molten cheese, about 30–35 minutes.

Hot-smoked salmon kedgeree with quails' eggs

This is a great favourite, and it can be served with hollandaise sauce, if you like (see below), which makes it a slightly more elegant dish. We always used to make and serve this kedgeree as one of our New Year's Morning Brunch dishes at Kinloch. Now we offer it every day as part of our breakfast menu. The very small amount of curry powder in the recipe is barely discernible as such, but its presence adds greatly to the overall delicious result.

Serves 6

1.2l (2 pints) milk
2 crumbled cubes of vegetable stock powder or jelly
75g (3oz) butter
1 tablespoon olive oil
4 banana shallots, diced finely
1 fairly level teaspoon medium-strength curry powder
375g (12oz) long grain rice – I use Basmati, as I prefer its flavour
675g (1½lb) hot-smoked salmon, flaked and skin discarded
12 quails' eggs, boiled for 5 minutes, then shelled and halved
About 15 grinds of black pepper
2 tablespoons finely chopped parsley

Start by heating the milk. Once warm, stir in the vegetable stock till dissolved.

In a wide sauté pan, melt 50g (2oz) of butter with the tablespoon of olive oil. Fry the finely diced shallots for 3–4 minutes, stirring continuously, then add the curry powder. Stir well, then mix in the rice. Pour in the hot stock/milk – it should come to about 2cm (1in.) above the level of the rice. Don't stir again: let the liquid bubble in the pan, cover with a tea towel, then with its lid, and cook on a gentle heat for 5 minutes. Lift the pan off the heat and leave for 20 minutes. By this time, the liquid should have been absorbed by the rice. Dice the remaining 25g (1oz) of butter and, with a fork, stir in with the flaked hot-smoked salmon. Reheat gently. Just before serving, season with pepper and parsley, and add the quails' eggs.

Hollandaise sauce
This luscious sauce can be served with the kedgeree recipe, elevating it to dinner-party food. Hollandaise need not be last-minute cooking; in fact, almost nothing bar a soufflé should ever need to be last-minute for the cook. This sauce keeps warm very well in a Thermos flask.

HOI!

Serves 6

3 large egg yolks
175g (6oz) butter, cut into 6 bits
1 level teaspoon salt
10 grinds of black pepper
2 tablespoons lemon juice – have a third to hand in case your
    taste dictates a sharper flavour for the sauce

Heat the lemon juice in a small pan on a very gentle heat.

Beat the yolks in a Pyrex bowl fitted snugly into a saucepan containing a small amount of simmering water. Add two bits of butter to the bowl and stir as the bowl heats from the water beneath it. The butter will melt and the combination of yolks and butter will form an emulsion. Add the rest of butter, a bit at a time, along with the salt and black pepper, stirring constantly – I use a flat metal whisk. About halfway through adding the butter, stir in one tablespoon of warmed lemon juice, then the second, and when all the butter is incorporated and the sauce is thick, carefully – so as not to scald your arm from the steam beneath the bowl – lift the bowl of hollandaise sauce off the heat. Taste, and stir in the third tablespoon of lemon juice, if you think it is needed. Pour the sauce into a Thermos flask. Alternatively, put the bowl of sauce in a warm place – but *not* on direct heat – and serve fairly soon.

Salmon in saffron and shallot sauce

I like to serve boiled Basmati rice with this, and green vegetables, such as roast courgettes. The sauce can be made a day in advance, then reheated, the cut-up raw salmon added 2–3 minutes before serving. It is a most convenient as well as delicious main course for a special occasion.

Serves 6

unsmoked salmon – weighing approx. 175g (6oz) per person

For the sauce:
6 banana shallots – the large, oval-shaped shallots with a slightly violet coloured flesh, diced finely
300ml (½ pint) dry white wine – I use a sauvignon blanc
450ml (¾ pint) vegetable stock
½ teaspoon saffron strands
½ teaspoon salt
About 15 grinds of black pepper
300ml (½ pint) double cream – it must be double!
1 tablespoon finely chopped parsley

Put the finely diced shallots into a saucepan with the wine and stock. Bring to a gentle simmer. When the liquid has reduced by about two-thirds, add the saffron, salt and black pepper and stir in the double cream. Bring the contents of the pan back to a simmer and continue to cook until the sauce is fairly thick – about the

consistency of pouring cream. If you are making this in
advance, remove the sauce from the heat at this stage and
store in a cool place.

Add the salmon 2 or 3 minutes before serving,
which will be enough time for the salmon to cook
through in the hot sauce. Add the finely chopped parsley
to finish off the dish.

Stir-fried salmon with lime, ginger, spring onions and sugarsnap peas

This is one of those quick dishes where time is spent in the preparation, which can be done in advance: given a really sharp knife, the preparation takes only a few minutes. You can use either fresh salmon or slightly smoked salmon fillets – whichever you prefer and can get hold of.

I like to serve this with Basmati rice, with a table-spoon of olive oil and one of finely chopped parsley stirred in, as both give the cooked rice a more appealing appearance.

Serves 6

8 salmon fillets, each weighing 175g (6oz), skinned and
    sliced into fine strips 1cm wide
4 tablespoons olive oil
24 (approx.) spring onions, trimmed and sliced into 4–5 pieces
4cm (2in.) root ginger, skin pared off and diced finely
1–2 fat cloves of garlic, diced
450g (1lb) sugarsnap peas, sliced diagonally – each into
    no fewer than 5 strips
finely grated rind of 2 limes, both well washed and dried before
    grating (washing removes the preservative)
1 teaspoon salt
About 20 grinds of black pepper
About ¼ teaspoon grated dried chilli – optional

Heat the olive oil in a wide sauté pan over a high heat. Stir-fry the salmon strips until they are completely opaque. When you cut a strip in half, it should be cooked through. Scoop the cooked salmon into a warm bowl.

Stir-fry the diced ginger and garlic, the spring onions and sugarsnap peas for about 5 minutes. Return the salmon to the pan and at the same time stir in the grated lime rinds, the salt and pepper, and, if you are including it, the chilli.

Salmon, asparagus and lemon risotto

Serves 6

3 tablespoons olive oil
2 medium-sized onions, finely diced
450g (1lb) risotto rice, either Arborio or Carnaroli
150ml (¼ pint) dry white wine
1.2l (2½ pints) stock, either vegetable or chicken
450g (1lb) asparagus, British or, better still, grown as near
    to where you live as possible
50g (2oz) butter, diced
Finely grated rind of 1 lemon
1 teaspoon salt
About 20 grinds of black pepper
675g (1½lb) salmon, skin removed and cut into
    dice about 1cm in size

In a sauté pan, heat the olive oil and fry the onions over a moderate heat for about 5 minutes, stirring from time to time, until they are quite soft and transparent-looking. They shouldn't turn colour. During this time, prepare the asparagus – trim off the tough ends and slice the remainder of each stalk on the diagonal into

pieces about half a centimetre thick. Leave the spears whole unless they are very large, in which case slice them too.

Once the onions are softened, add in the rice. Stir on the same moderate heat for 2–3 minutes – the aim is to coat each grain with olive oil. Then add the dry white wine. Let this bubble away before adding some of the stock. Stir, then let the rice and stock simmer very gently until the liquid has almost evaporated. At this stage, add in the trimmed asparagus and more stock. Simmer gently, stirring occasionally, before adding more stock, stirring well, simmering to evaporate the liquid, then adding more stock. Continue until not quite all of the stock is used up. Mix in the lemon rind, salt and pepper, and stir in the butter. This gives the risotto a gloss but also the flavour of the butter, which is so complementary to that of the asparagus and the hint of lemon. Stir in the remaining stock just before serving, at which point the diced salmon is added as well. This will cook within a minute or two at the most in the heat of the risotto. The rice shouldn't be at all stodgy, rather slightly sloppy.

Double salmon fish pie

I think that smoked fish is imperative in any fish pie and for this salmon version I use a combination of plain salmon and the slightly smoked salmon fillets to be found in any good supermarket's fish department. This is such a good fish pie.

The celeriac in the potato is a matter of choice – if you don't like celeriac, just leave it out and use purely potato mash. But the seasoning for the mash matters a great deal in the success of the whole dish.

And whereas we love chopped hard-boiled eggs in a fish pie, I'm sure that you all know *not* to include the hard-boiled eggs if you want to make and freeze this recipe: once frozen, hard-boiled eggs become the kind of rubber product Dunlop would be proud to produce – but which renders the fish pie inedible!

FAULT

Serves 6

For the filling:
50g (2oz) butter, melted
1 tablespoon olive oil
1 onion, finely diced
1 stick of celery, peeled with a potato peeler to remove the
    stringy bits, then sliced finely
2 rounded tablespoons plain flour
750ml (1¼ pints) milk
1 teaspoon salt
About 15 grinds of black pepper
A good grating of nutmeg
450g (1lb) slightly smoked raw salmon fillets, skin and any
    bones removed, cut into chunks as for the unsmoked salmon
450g (1lb) plain salmon, skin and bones removed, and
    cut into chunks of about 1cm (½in.)
3 hard-boiled eggs, chopped

For the celeriac/potato mash:
450g (1lb) potatoes (I usually buy Rooster) weighed when peeled.
    Cut into even-sized chunks
½ celeriac, skin cut off and cut into chunks even in
    size to the potato
300ml (½ pint) milk
50g (2oz) butter
1 teaspoon salt
About 12 grinds of black pepper

To begin the filling, heat the butter and olive oil together,
then fry the onion and celery over a moderate heat for

about four minutes. Stir in the flour and cook for a minute before gradually adding the milk, stirring all the time. Let the sauce simmer for two minutes, then take the pan off the heat and mix in the salt, black pepper and nutmeg, and the small pieces of both types of salmon. The fish will cook in the heat of the sauce. Finally, add in the chopped hard-boiled eggs.

Tip the contents of the pan into an ovenproof dish and allow to cool.

Peel and chop the potatoes and celeriac, then boil together in salted water until tender. Drain and steam, then mash well. Beat in the milk, butter and seasoning with a wooden spoon, then spoon the mash evenly over the surface of the cooled salmon in its sauce. With a fork, draw lines over the entire surface.

Bake in a moderate heat (350°F/180°C/gas 4) until the sauce bubbles slightly around the edges of the mash and the surface of the mash turns very slightly browned – about 35–40 minutes (from room temperature, as opposed to straight from the fridge – always take the dish into room temperature for about half an hour before putting it into the oven).

NB this fish pie can be made 24 hours in advance of reheating to serve, but cover the surface with cling film before putting it, cooled, into the fridge.

Coulibiac

A proper coulibiac contains rice and mushrooms within the puff pastry encasing the salmon and, immodest though it sounds, I much prefer my own version, which contains neither rice (so stodgy and unnecessary with puff pastry) nor mushrooms, which in my opinion don't particularly complement either the taste or texture of salmon in any form.

Coulibiac is absolutely not the fiddle that people suppose it to be. For a special occasion, it is positively convenient because it can be made in its entirety a day in advance, then kept (covered with cling film) in the fridge until 30 minutes before baking. I do practise what I preach because I made this for both my Skye grandsons' christenings on two separate occasions; on the first, I was so grateful that I *had* made this because I had a frantic phone call from a fellow parishioner who had gone into the

church early on the day of the christening only to find a huge flower arrangement that I had done the previous day flat on its face on the floor – top heavy – it had toppled over! So with the lunch I was serving after the service completely under control, I could nip into Broadford and redo the flowers, clearing up the mess on the floor as I went! The coulibiac tasted even better knowing just *how* convenient it had been!

Below the recipe, I have added instructions for making the sauce to go with coulibiac. This, too, can be made a day in advance and reheated to serve with the sliced coulibiac.

———————

Serves 6 – just double and treble everything to serve more

900g (2lb) filleted salmon, skinned and all bones removed
50g (2oz) butter

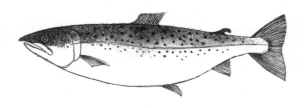

4 banana shallots, diced finely
1 teaspoon salt
About 15 grinds of black pepper
1 cucumber, both ends sliced off and the cucumber peeled with a
        potato peeler, then cut into chunks about 2in./4cm and each
        chunk halved. Remove the seeds from each half, then finely
        and neatly dice the seedless cucumber flesh
Finely grated rind of 1 lemon
675g (1½lb) puff pastry – I buy either Bell's or Saxby's
1 egg, beaten

Melt the butter in a wide saucepan and fry the shallots, stirring occasionally, for 4–5 minutes. Add the prepared cucumber. Add to the shallots in the pan and, stirring occasionally, fry them altogether for a further 3–4 minutes. Take the pan off the heat and stir in the finely grated lemon rind, the salt and black pepper, and leave to cool.

Roll out two-thirds of the puff pastry into an oblong bigger than the filleted salmon. Put this onto a non-stick large roasting tin or baking tray. Place the salmon on the rolled-out pastry and spoon the cooled shallot/cucumber mixture on top, smoothing it into an even layer all over the fish.

Roll out the remainder of the puff pastry, big enough to cover the salmon, and place it on top. Brush the pastry with beaten egg and seal the edges, encasing the salmon completely. Slash the top of the pastry in four or five places – to release steam as it bakes – and, if you like, garnish with pastry fish. Brush the whole thing all over with beaten egg.

Bake in a hot oven (400°F/200°C/gas 6) for 30–35 minutes or until the pastry is golden brown and well puffed up. With two fish slices, lift the coulibiac onto a warmed serving dish. Slice thickly to serve.

Sauce to accompany coulibiac

---

3 banana shallots, finely diced
300ml (½ pint) good white wine – I use a sauvignon blanc
Finely grated rind of 1 lemon
300ml (½ pint) double cream
1 teaspoon salt
About 10 grinds of black pepper

Put the finely diced shallots into a saucepan and add the wine. Simmer gently until the wine has almost disappeared. Add the finely grated lemon rind, the salt and black pepper, and the double cream. Simmer, but remember that the longer the sauce simmers, the thicker it will become. I suggest a minute or two, no longer. Reheat to serve.

Baked fillet of salmon with carrot, shallot and ginger timbales

The salmon in this recipe is steam-baked between two sheets of baking parchment. This is one of the best ways to cook salmon – or any other fish, for that matter. The ginger carrot timbales are an elegant way to serve the fish with a vegetable, but I still like to add a green vegetable to complete this main course; for example sugarsnap peas stir-fried with some garlic and grated lemon rind are an ideal accompaniment to the smooth carrot timbales.

The timbales mixture can also be made a day in advance, which is most convenient, but be sure to give the mixture a good stir before pouring it into the buttered ramekins to bake.

For the salmon:
6 pieces of filleted salmon, each weighing about 175g (6oz)
175g (6oz) butter, cut into 6 even pieces
Salt
Black pepper

To prepare the salmon for baking, lay a sheet of baking parchment on a baking sheet and place the pieces of filleted salmon onto this. Put one piece of butter on each piece of salmon, season with salt and black pepper, then cover with a second sheet of parchment, tucking it under the fish to form a sort of parcel. Bake in a moderate heat

(350°F/180°C/gas 4) for 15–20 minutes or until, when you unwrap the parchment and gently prise apart the thickest part of one piece of salmon, the fish falls into opaque flakes. If it still looks raw, re-wrap the parchment and bake for longer.

For the timbales:
4 tablespoons olive oil
4 banana shallots, chopped
900g (2lbs) carrots, weighed before peeling, diced fairly small
2in./5cm approx piece of ginger, skin cut off and the ginger
    cut into chunks
600ml (1 pint) stock, either vegetable or chicken
1 teaspoon salt
About 15 grinds of black pepper
A grating of nutmeg
Finely grated rind of 1 lemon
150ml (¼ pint) double cream
3 large eggs

Heat the olive oil in a large saucepan and fry the shallots for 3–4 minutes, then add the ginger and carrots to the pan. Stir well and cook for a further 3–4 minutes, stirring occasionally. Add the stock, salt, black pepper and nutmeg to the pan and simmer gently, stirring occasionally, until the liquid has virtually reduced right away. Take the pan off the heat and cool. Tip the contents of the pan into a food processor and whizz, adding the eggs, one by one, the grated lemon rind and, lastly, the cream. Whizz briefly once the cream is added. Scrape the contents of the processor into a measure jug. Store in the fridge, covered, until you are ready to bake the timbales.

Brush out six large ramekins with olive oil. Stir up the ginger–carrot mixture and divide it evenly between the oiled ramekins. Put in a roasting tin with nearly boiling water coming halfway up the sides of the ramekins and bake in a moderate heat (350°F/180°C/gas 4) for 30–35 minutes, or until the tops of the timbales feel firm when gently pressed. Take them out of the oven and leave to stand for 10–15 minutes.

To turn them out, run a knife around the inside of each ramekin and shake one onto each of six warmed plates. Serve a piece of baked salmon beside each timbale.

Salmon quenelles

The very word 'quenelle' used to make my eyes glaze over; I imagined they were something I could never tackle, that they were way beyond my ability. Then, some years ago, when doing a cooking demonstration in Pitlochry Theatre, I went to stay with Henrietta Thewes and she made the most delectable and delicious salmon quenelles; she made me realise that they *are* do-able, even by me. They are so good that I've been making them ever since!

For this recipe, you can use slightly smoked salmon fillets instead of plain salmon, if you prefer.

I have added the recipe for a creamy tomato sauce below which I love to use as an accompaniment.

Serves 6

675g (1½lb) salmon, skin removed and cut into small chunks
1 large egg, plus 2 large egg whites
300ml (½ pint) double cream
1 teaspoon Tabasco
15 grinds of black pepper
About 1 litre of vegetable stock (in which to cook the quenelles)

Put the salmon into a food processor and whizz, adding the egg, egg whites, Tabasco, black pepper and double cream. Scrape the contents of the processor into a bowl, cover with cling film and leave in the fridge for several hours or overnight.

Heat the stock to a depth of about 8cm (3in.) in a wide sauté pan. Bring to a rolling boil. With two tablespoons, shape the chilled salmon mixture into egg shapes, the traditional quenelle shape, and poach in the fast-boiling stock. They will take five minutes and need to be turned over during that time.

Butter a wide ovenproof dish. Place the cooked quenelles on this when their cooking time finishes.

Creamy tomato sauce

Serves 6

25g (1oz) butter
2 tablespoons olive oil
1 red onion, diced
8 ripe tomatoes, skinned, halved, seeds scooped away
     and flesh diced
Juice of 1 lemon
1 teaspoon salt
About 15 grinds of black pepper
300ml (½ pint) double cream

Heat the olive oil and butter together in a saucepan and fry the diced red onion, stirring, for 3–4 minutes. Then add the neatly diced tomato flesh to the pan, along with the salt, black pepper and lemon juice. Cook for a couple of minutes and then add the double cream to the pan. Stir well and simmer for 2–3 minutes.

Pour the sauce over the quenelles, loosely cover with foil and keep warm in a low temperature oven before serving.

This is good with crispy potatoes roasted with rosemary and a green vegetable – my favourite is sugarsnap peas, steamed but still crunchy.

Barbecued salmon

We love to barbecue salmon. I have to say that we have a
good old-fashioned charcoal barbecue – none of that
gas-fired (to my mind) pseudo-chargrilling for us! The
foil wrapping prevents the salmon from drying out
during this most drying form of cooking – and it also
allows seasonings – in the form of salt, pepper and lemon,
as well as olive oil – to be barbecued with the fish itself.
By slashing the foil wrapping, the flavour of the charcoal
can penetrate the fish as it cooks, too.

I tend to serve the tomato and blanched garlic
mayonnaise as an accompaniment to barbecued salmon,
as it is the one most frequently asked for.

_____

Serves 6

1.2kg (2½lbs) filleted salmon, skin on
1 rounded teaspoon salt
About 15 grinds of black pepper
1 lemon, washed and dried to remove the preservative,
    very thinly sliced
2 tablespoons extra virgin olive oil
75g (3oz) parsley

_____

Put a piece of foil much larger than the piece of salmon
onto a plastic tray (easy for transporting to the barbecue,
and remember to take with you a warmed dish to serve
the fish on once cooked) slashing the foil in several

places before putting the salmon onto the foil, skin down.

Rub the olive oil into the fish, then season with salt and black pepper. Lay the thinly sliced lemon in a layer over the surface of the fish, then strew the parsley on top of the lemon slices. Scrimp together the foil above the fish, as for a Cornish pasty.

Put the foil parcel onto the grill above white-hot coals and leave to cook for 20 minutes. Open the top of the foil and, with two forks, gently prise apart the thickest part of the salmon: if it falls into opaque flakes, it is cooked; if it still looks a bit raw, seal up the foil once more and continue to cook for a further several minutes before checking again.

Tomato and garlic mayonnaise

Serves 6

2 fat cloves of garlic in their skins, put into a small saucepan
    and covered with water, brought to the boil, water drained
    off and the garlic immersed in fresh cold water, brought to
    the boil then drained off once more. Skin the garlic cloves
1 large egg, plus 1 large egg yolk
1 teaspoon caster sugar
1 rounded teaspoon salt
About 12 grinds of black pepper
1 rounded teaspoon Dijon mustard
300ml (½ pint) olive oil

2/3 tablespoons white wine vinegar
4 ripe tomatoes, skinned, halved, seeds scooped out,
      then neatly diced

_____

Put the skinned garlic into a food processor and add the
egg, the egg yolk, the sugar, salt, black pepper and
mustard and whizz, adding the oil, drop by drop, until
you have an emulsion, then add the oil in a thin, steady
trickle. When all the oil is incorporated, whizz in two
tablespoons of white wine vinegar, taste and add a third
tablespoon if desired. Scrape the mayonnaise into a bowl
and mix in the diced tomatoes. Cover the bowl and store
the mayonnaise in a cool place, or the fridge, until you
are ready to serve.

Seared pepper-crusted salmon fillets with mango and mint salsa

This may sound a bit odd, but it is delicious. The Demerara sugar, with the salt and parsley, forms the simple crust, which is pressed into the skin, and the fillets are then seared in a small amount of olive oil in a non-stick sauté pan over a very high heat. This is the only dish

in which I can eat the salmon skin! It is so good for you but is normally too thick and chewy for my taste. Here, it is meltingly crispy.

The mango and mint salsa, with finely sliced spring onions, complements the flavour of the seared salmon perfectly. We might take a lesson from the Italians, who use mint much more than we tend to – and with fish recipes.

Serves 6

6 pieces of filleted salmon, skin on, each weighing about 175g (6oz)

For the crust:
50g (2oz) parsley, stalks discarded, chopped moderately finely
2 rounded tablespoons Demerara sugar
1 rounded teaspoon salt
30 grinds of coarsely ground black pepper – alternatively
    put 2 teaspoons of black peppercorns into a pestle and
    mortar and pound to crush them
2–3 tablespoons olive oil, for cooking the fillets

In a bowl, mix together the chopped parsley, Demerara sugar, salt and black pepper, mixing thoroughly. Divide this between the six fillets of salmon, pressing it as firmly as you can over the skin of each.

Heat the olive oil in a sauté pan over a high heat until the oil is smoking hot, then put the pieces of salmon into the pan skin down. There will be a lot of smoke initially – but don't be tempted to move the pieces of salmon in the pan for 2–3 minutes; you must let the sugar caramelise the crust onto the skin of the fillets. You should be able to see the fish cook above the skin – if you are in any doubt, with two forks gently part the thickest section of one of the fillets to check that the flakes look opaque. If it looks raw, continue cooking.

Lift the fillets onto a warmed serving plate, and serve with the following simple salsa.

Mango and Mint Salsa
This salsa benefits from being made several hours in advance.

Serves 6

2 ripe mangos, peeled and the flesh diced as finely as you can –
    difficult, if the mango is as ripe as it should be!
3 spring onions, trimmed and very finely sliced
8 large mint leaves, preferably applemint, which has the
    best flavour of all the mint varieties, very finely sliced
1 lime, its rind finely grated and its juice

Combine all the above ingredients thoroughly in a bowl. Serve a spoonful beside each piece of salmon.

Steam-baked salmon with pak choi, ginger and garlic

This is a light salmon main course but the flavours make a great impact, combining ginger, garlic and lemongrass. This recipe could so easily feature on WeightWatchers — and should do! You can substitute young spinach for the pak choi, if you prefer.

Serves 6

6 pieces of filleted salmon, each weighing about 175g (6oz)
3 heads of pak choi, finely sliced
4cm (2in.) root ginger, skin pared off and very finely diced
2 fat cloves of garlic, skinned and very finely diced
1 teaspoon salt
About 12 grinds of black pepper
2 stalks of lemongrass, bashed with a rolling pin, to release the flavour

Line a baking tray with a sheet of baking parchment. Put the pieces of salmon onto this, close together. In a bowl, put the finely sliced pak choi, diced ginger and garlic, salt and black pepper, and mix thoroughly. Spoon this mixture on top of the salmon and lay the lemongrass on top. Cover with a second sheet of baking parchment, tucking it under the fish to make a parcel. Bake in a moderate heat (350°F/180°C/gas 4) for 25–30 minutes. This is good served with couscous with olive oil, grated lime and chopped parsley stirred through it.

Hot-smoked salmon fishcakes

No fishcake is worth eating unless it is made with smoked fish. A combination of plain fish and potato – even if the fish is salmon – makes for dismal eating indeed. However fishcakes made with hot-smoked salmon are positively luxurious – and so delicious. They are convenient, too, in that they can be made up to 48 hours ahead of being fried and eaten. They can also be

frozen, but for a very limited time only (no more than 5–7 days).

What you serve with them is up to you: tomato ketchup, hollandaise sauce, or the creamy tomato sauce I serve with the salmon quenelles on p. 90. All are delicious!

I find the Rooster variety of potato ideal for this – and for pretty well everything else, as well!

Serves 6

900g (2lb) potatoes, weighed when peeled, cut into chunks,
    boiled in salted water till tender and mashed very thoroughly,
    then cooled
1 teaspoon salt
About 15 grinds of black pepper
A grating of nutmeg
675g (1½lb) hot-smoked salmon, flaked from skin
1 large egg, beaten on a plate
4 rounded tablespoons flour, sieved onto a plate
2–3 rounded tablespoons finely chopped parsley

Beat the salt, black pepper and nutmeg into the mashed potatoes – you can do this either when mashing or when the mash has cooled. Add the flaked hot-smoked salmon to the potatoes, and mix very well.

Line a baking tray with a sheet of baking parchment.

With your hands, divide the potato/salmon mixture into even-sized small balls and shape them into fishcakes. Dip each first in flour, then beaten egg, and lastly into the parsley. Place them onto the baking parchment.

When you are ready to cook them, put two table-spoons of olive oil into a wide non-stick sauté pan over a fairly high heat. Once the fishcakes are in the pan, do not be tempted to move them around. Leave them for two minutes and then turn over to cook on the other side. They should form a crispy parsley crust – fried parsley tastes so good. As they are cooked, lift the fishcakes onto an ovenproof dish lined with a couple of thicknesses of absorbent kitchen paper. Keep them warm till you are ready to serve them, with a green vegetable or a mixed leaf salad.

Creamy salmon, shallot, spinach and saffron stew

This is a luxurious main course, needing only as accompaniment either very well mashed potatoes or warmed crusty granary or seeded bread. Don't have a fit at the cream in the list of ingredients: just remember that no one person is going to consume the whole amount – divided by six it is almost negligible!
This is quick, and very, very good to eat.

Serves 6

2–3 tablespoons olive oil
6 banana shallots, sliced finely
450g (1lb) young spinach leaves
2 generous pinches of saffron strands
600ml (1 pint) double cream – and it must be double!
900g (2lb) slightly smoked salmon fillets, skin removed and
    sliced into 1cm thick slices
About 15 grinds of black pepper
No need for salt

In a wide saucepan, heat the olive oil and, over a moderate heat, fry the finely sliced shallots, stirring occasionally, until they are completely soft, about 6–7 minutes. Add the spinach, saffron and cream to the pan, then grind in the black pepper. Clamp on the lid and the spinach will wilt quickly, in about a minute. Add the sliced salmon, stir it through the contents of the pan and let the cream simmer gently, as the fish cooks in the heat, for about 2–3 minutes.

Serve ladled into warmed soup plates.

DOUBLE CREAM

SAFFRON

Trout

RAINBOW TROUT

BROWN TROUT

The only fresh-water fish which, to my mind, is worth eating is trout. It has the potential to be delicious – and it can be cooked in a variety of ways.

The fresher the trout, the better it tastes, as I'm sure any angler will testify. The best trout I've eaten are those we buy when staying with our daughter and her family during their holidays in their Austrian home, where a visit to Frau Gottsbacker to buy trout is a regular occurrence. I'm not

sure quite how well Frau Gottsbacker's methods of killing the trout would go down in the UK, though, where many people tend to be a bit squeamish about such things. She fishes them out of a holding pool beside the beautiful river where she lives and, clasping the live fish, she bashes its head on a rock until it is lifeless. Usually one sharp bash does the trick. We then take them home and cook them. They are the very best.

TRAUT
FRAU
GOTTSBACKER

Butter-fried trout with flaked almonds and halved grapes

Serves 6

6 trout, cleaned (i.e. gutted)
3 tablespoons plain flour, sieved
120g (4oz) butter
120g (4oz) flaked almonds
1 rounded teaspoon salt
About 15 grinds of black pepper
220g (8oz) seedless grapes, preferably black, each cut in half
1½ lemons

In a wide sauté pan, melt half the amount of butter and fry the flaked almonds, salt and black pepper over a moderately high heat, stirring regularly, until the almonds become a pale biscuit colour. Add the halved grapes to the almonds in the pan and continue to cook together for a further five minutes. Then, using a slotted spoon and leaving behind as much of the butter as you can, scoop out the almonds and grapes and put them into a warmed bowl.

In the same pan, melt the rest of the butter. Dip each trout on either side in the sieved flour and fry for two minutes on each side.

Serve with a quarter of lemon at the side and with a good spoonful of the fried almonds and grapes over each fish.

Trout baked with lemon, parsley and chives

This is a light way to cook and eat trout. It is simplicity itself to prepare, scarcely deserving the title of 'recipe', but worth including for the very good reason that it *is* so simple!

Serves 6

6 trout, cleaned
2 lemons
1 rounded teaspoon salt
About 12 grinds of black pepper
2 tablespoons olive oil
2 rounded tablespoons parsley, finely chopped
1 tablespoon snipped chives

Lay a sheet of foil on a roasting tin and put the trout side by side onto this. Half the lemons and squeeze the juice over the trout. Scatter with the herbs and season. Cover with a second piece of foil and scrimp the edges together at the sides to make a parcel. Bake in a moderate heat (350°F/180°C/gas 4) for 40 minutes. Open the parcel and serve each trout on a warmed plate, the juices from the parcel spooned over each trout.

Smoked trout and lime pâté

For this, I use hot-smoked trout. It is definitely worth spending the small time it takes to pick out the numerous tiny bones because an almost bone-free pâté is so much nicer to eat than if the texture bears a resemblance to a pin cushion. This makes a good first course, but it can equally be used to fill sandwiches or buns for a picnic.

Serves 6

3 hot-smoked trout, filleted and de-boned carefully
375g (12oz) cream cheese, which can be half-fat, if you prefer
1 teaspoon horseradish – my preference is for Colman's or
    the Co-op's own brand
Finely grated rind of 1 lime and 2 tablespoons lime juice
No need for salt, but 12 grinds of black pepper
50g (2oz) parsley, tough stalks discarded

Put the flaked hot-smoked trout into a food processor, adding the cream cheese, horseradish, lime rind and juice, and black pepper. Whizz till smooth, then add the parsley – the flecks of green lift the colour and make this pâté, which tastes so good, visually more appealing.

Sweet-and-sour baked trout

Cooking trout in this way gives it a slight oriental kick. It is so simple to prepare and light in its content.

Serves 6

6 trout, cleaned
2 tablespoons soy sauce
6 spring onions, trimmed and sliced finely
1 piece of root ginger, approx. 4cm (2in.), skin cut off and finely diced
2 fat cloves of garlic, skinned and finely diced
1 tablespoon toasted sesame oil
300ml (½ pint) vegetable stock
1 teaspoon caster sugar
About 12 grinds of black pepper – no need for salt, the soy sauce contributes enough
Finely grated rind and juice of 1 lime

Combine all of the ingredients except the trout in a wide sauté pan and bring to a gentle simmer. Put the trout into the pan and cover with its lid. Cook over a gentle heat for 10–15 minutes, turning over each trout during the cooking time.